AF131427

BOOK ANALYSIS

By Angela Youngman

The Wife of Bath's Tale

BY GEOFFREY CHAUCER

GEOFFREY CHAUCER

BRITISH WRITER

- **Born in London c. 1343.**
- **Died in London in 1400.**
- **Notable works:**
  - *The Canterbury Tales* (c. 1380s), narrative poetry
  - *Parlement of Foules* (c. 1380s), poetry
  - *Troilus and Criseyde* (c. 1380s), poetry

A medieval courtier, diplomat, lawyer and civil servant, Chaucer travelled around Western Europe on the King's business. Although he held a fairly high position within the Court, Chaucer did not come from an aristocratic family. His grandfather ran a tavern in the town of Ipswich, before moving to London and becoming a merchant. His parents were wine merchants living in the City of London. Chaucer is believed to have married Philippa de Roet, a lady-in-waiting to Constance of Castile (Spanish duchess, 1354-1394), the second wife of John of Gaunt (English duke, 1340-1399). He started his seminal work,

The Canterbury Tales, during the 1380s, and it was incomplete at his death. *The Canterbury Tales* have never been out of print and have constantly influenced writers, artists and filmmakers ever since. The stories have a perennial appeal. *The Canterbury Tales* have also been a key influence on the development of the English language. Just like William Shakespeare (English playwright, 1564-1616), Chaucer was receptive to new ideas and the sheer variety and versatility of English. Many of the words he used were relatively new to the English language, often being taken from other languages including Greek, Latin and Arabic.

THE WIFE OF BATH'S TALE

ARTHURIAN STORY

- **Genre:** poetry
- **Reference edition:** Chaucer, G. (1992) *The Canterbury Tales.* London: Everyman.
- **1st edition:** late 1380s (exact date unknown)
- **Themes:** sex and marriage, feminism, authority and control, pilgrimage

Written in the first person, *The Wife of Bath's Tale* focuses on issues of love, romance and relationships between men and women. It is divided into two sections: the Prologue, which includes a physical description of the Wife of Bath as well as biographical details about her, and the fictional story that she recounts to the other pilgrims. The story is set in the court of King Arthur and Queen Guinevere, and focuses on the activities of a young knight who rapes a pretty maiden. For his crime, he is condemned to death by decapitation. The Queen offers him one chance to save his life: he has to leave the Court, travel the world and discover what women want most before returning with his answer. If he cannot find the correct answer, he will die. A long search and difficult choices results in the discovery that what women want most is sovereignty over men.

SUMMARY

The Prologue is the autobiography of the Wife of Bath herself, highlighting her personal beliefs and attitudes. She has had five husbands, enabling her life to be governed by experience rather than authority. She cannot understand why Christ reproached a woman for having five husbands, since it is important to follow the Old Testament command to 'go forth and multiply'. She further justifies her point of view by pointing out that King Solomon had many wives, and St Paul said it was better to marry than suffer lust. She also argues that fulfilling sexual needs is pleasurable as well as a basic function, and she has enjoyed having sex. After discussing her first four husbands, she explains how she gained control over Jankyn, her fifth husband. They met during the funeral of her fourth husband, and married within a month. When Jankyn insisted on reading tales about unfaithful women to her, stressing their disgraceful behaviour, she grabbed the book and hit him with it. Jankyn fell into the fire. Jumping up, he hit her. The Wife of Bath pretended he had killed her. When he bent over to look at her, she hit him, then pretended to die again. This upset Jankyn so much that he promised he would do anything she liked if she chose to live. This was how she gained 'sovereignty' over her husband, and they lived happily until his death. Her story aims to reinforce these views on marriage and authority with a story that mirrors her experiences.

THE RAPE

A young knight encounters a pretty maiden and rapes her. When the crime becomes known, the knight is condemned to die by decapitation. Queen Guinevere and her ladies take pity on him and advise King Arthur to give him a chance to save his life. Bowing to his wife's advice, the King agrees. Queen Guinevere issues a decree that the young knight must discover what women want most. He must return to the court with his answer within a year. If no answer is found, or the answer is wrong, then the knight will die.

THE SEARCH FOR ANSWERS

While travelling, the knight asks every woman he meets: What do you want most? He is dismayed when every answer is different. Money, honour, friendship, appearance, discretion, sex, marriage, and children are among the many answers he is given. Some say that they just want to be able to do as they please. Others prefer to be secretive – although the Wife of Bath says this is impossible, citing the story of Midas and the Ass's Ears as proof that women cannot keep secrets.

By the end of the year, the knight is no closer to finding an answer. Riding back to King Arthur's court, he encounters a group of women dancing in a forest and asks his question. They disappear and he suddenly finds himself facing a 'loathsome hag' who asks if she can help him. The knight explains his predicament, saying he will reward her in any way she chooses if she can help. She tells him that she knows the answer, but in return for her help, he must promise to marry her. Reluctantly, the knight agrees.

THE MARRIAGE

Arriving at King Arthur's Court, the knight tells the Queen that what women want most is quite simple – control of any relationship with a husband or lovers. The Queen agrees. Then the hag demands that the knight fulfil his promise by marrying her immediately. He is reluctant but has no choice.

When they go to bed that night, his new wife asks why he is unhappy. He tells her the truth – she is ugly, unpleasant, of low birth, and he is ashamed of her. His wife does not take offence, merely asking whether true 'gentilesse'' (nobility of character) is hereditary. She points out that it is not unknown for sons of noble fathers to be evil, even though they share the same bloodline. Similarly, her family may be of low status, but that does not necessarily make her evil. She argues that real riches and 'gentilesse' come from having nothing and wanting nothing, whereas real poverty is caused by covetousness.

THE DECISION

She offers him a choice. She can transform herself to become young and pretty, but also flirtatious and unfaithful; or she can stay ugly, loyal and good. The knight decides that he will leave the choice to her. In doing so, he gives her what she most desires: the authority to make her own choice, thus controlling the nature of their relationship. In the final test of her power, she orders that he kiss her, even though he finds her unattractive. As he does so, she undergoes a transformation, becoming both beautiful and good, thus giving her husband what he most desires. These decisions result in a long and happy marriage in which the wife is loyal to her husband.

CHARACTER STUDY

THE WIFE OF BATH

The Wife of Bath is one of only two female storytellers within *The Canterbury Tales*, the other being the Prioress. Unlike the Prioress, the Wife of Bath is very much rooted in the secular world. She is rich, self-confident, sexually experienced, keen on travelling, and independent-minded. Since pilgrimages were the main reason for travelling to far-off places during the medieval period, the Wife of Bath has taken part in many pilgrimages. Her journeys have taken her to many European lands, including Santiago de Compostela in Spain. However, she is clear as to why she goes on pilgrimages: it is not for religious reasons, but as a way of exploring the world. She is, quite simply, a medieval tourist.

Her brightly coloured, extravagant, stylish, handmade clothes, complete with new soft leather shoes, reflect her personality, her skill as a seamstress and the extent of her wealth. Her stockings are scarlet – a very expensive dye sourced from individual beetles. Even the fact that she comes from Bath is an indicator of wealth. At the time *The Canterbury Tales* were written, Bath was a prosperous cloth-making town, which exported its fabrics all over Europe. She is intelligent and able to formulate clever arguments, even though her knowledge of the Bible and other books is sometimes flawed.

Marriage and male/female relationships are a subject upon which she possesses strong views. She has already been married five times, during which she has learned how to cope in a man's world. How far her accounts of her marriages are true, or to what extent they have been exaggerated in order to provide a good story and emphasise her point of view, is impossible to ascertain. She does admit that she is seeking to entertain her listeners.

Out of all the Pilgrims in *The Canterbury Tales*, the Wife of Bath is by far the most lively and instantly recognizable. It is a superb portrait of a woman who knows exactly what she wants, and is prepared to enjoy life no matter what happens.

In the General Prologue of *The Canterbury Tales*, Chaucer gives a physical description of the Wife of Bath, alongside all the other pilgrims. The Wife of Bath's description is given in lines 447-478. Her name is Alison, but this is rarely used at any point, being simply referred to as the Wife of Bath. The fact that she has a gap tooth is symbolic, as this was often used as a symbol for lust and sensuality. She is deaf in one ear, possibly a result of her fight with Jankyn, and is very well built. She enjoys being in the company of others, especially men.

THE KNIGHT

We are not given any specific details about the knight; merely that he is young, lusty and strong. Having committed the crime of rape, he has to make amends and is given a quest to discover what women really want. In doing so, he has to make difficult decisions about his own future. His fate rests on those decisions. By learning to respect women, and to acknowledge their rights and decisions, he gains his reward in the form of a loving, beautiful wife.

THE LOATHSOME HAG

A magical creature, she has the ability to transform herself. There is no explanation given as to how a group of maidens suddenly becomes one person, but at the end of the story it is the redeeming power of a kiss and the acceptance of a woman's control that turns her into a desirable, loving woman. She is never named, nor is there any specific description of her beyond the fact that she is unpleasant to look at, of low birth, and seemingly much older than the young knight (a reflection of the varying ages of Jankyn and the Wife of Bath). Her views on gentilesse and courtesy show she is able to argue her views and speak eloquently. She is also determined and insistent on getting her own way. She knows exactly what she wants – marriage to a knight – and is intent on achieving it.

ANALYSIS

HISTORICAL CONTEXT

In studying *The Wife of Bath's Tale*, it is important to remember the context in which it was written. This was just one of several stories within a collection known as *The Canterbury Tales*, which was written in the 14th century. During this period, the Church was coming under considerable criticism, and it is frequently the subject of mockery within the *Tales*. In *The Wife of Bath's Tale,* for example, the way in which the Wife jumbles up and uses inaccurate academic references mocks members of the Church who frequently sought to adapt or misuse Scripture in order to justify their actions. Other tales within the collection contain similar references to the problems within the Church, for example through the misbehaviour of various characters such as the Pardoner and the Prioress.

The Wife of Bath's Tale comprises two parts: the Prologue and the Story, both of which are designed to stress her views on marriage and authority. Although the story is outwardly a conventional Arthurian tale, it is designed to mirror the experiences of the Wife of Bath.

SEX

Within *The Wife of Bath's Tale*, sex and marriage dominate relationships between men and women. This is not just a matter of a physical relationship; rather, it reflects the prevalent attitudes towards authority and leadership. Men played a very dominant role in medieval society, with women being 'given' in marriage, and expected to obey their husbands.

The Wife of Bath outlines her experience of marriage. She has been married five times, with three 'good' marriages and two 'bad' ones. Her reasons for these classifications are simple: the first three were good because the husbands were rich, old and accepted her control. She would make countless accusations of infidelity until they were forced to give her what she wanted because of their apparent guilt. Sex was also used as a method of control. She openly admits to encouraging them in bed, but refusing full intercourse until they promised her money. Verbal tirades and sex forced her husband into submission. Nowadays, many would argue that this also demonstrated bullying, abusive behaviour.

In medieval times, women had very little real independence or power. It was only when widowed, or living in a convent, that they had some control over their lives. As a wealthy widow, the Wife of Bath was able to travel. Her experience of marriage had taught her how to control her husbands – by using her body as a bargaining tool. The Wife of Bath is very keen on sex, admitting she thoroughly enjoys it, and states that men owe women sex in marriage:

> "In wyfhod I wol use myn instrument
> As freely as my Makere hath it sent."
> (lines 155-156)

Her views were contrary to the teaching of the medieval Church, which believed that sex should only take place in order to create children. Instead, virginity and celibacy was praised, highlighting the number of saints who opted for death rather than marriage. The Wife of Bath points out that not everyone can be a virgin, as sex is the only way that virgins can be produced:

> "For hadde God commanded maydenhede
> Thane hadde he dampned weddyng with the dede;
> And certein, if ther were no seed ysowe,
> Viginitee, wherof thane sholde it grow?"
> (lines 75-78)

In her view, virginity should be left to those that wish to stay celibate but should not be enforced on others. It is a matter of personal choice. Other people should use their gifts, including their sexuality, as they wish. She quotes from the Bible, particularly relating to King Solomon, to show that the Bible does not condemn sexuality, even when it is outside the bounds of marriage.

Sexual elements are present within the Tale itself. The rape of a young girl causes the knight to be sent on a quest, and the story ends within the marital bed. Only when the knight gives his bride what she wants, accepting her as she is and being prepared to consummate the marriage, does the story reach a happy conclusion.

AUTHORITY AND CONTROL

This is a central theme within *The Wife of Bath's Tale*, linking to the other key theme of sex and marriage. *The Wife of Bath's Tale* is about control, authority and who should have control within a relationship of any kind. This control may be enforced through physical strength, as in the knight's rape of the maiden, through ideas such as Jankyn's views on women, or through female domination, as evidenced by the Wife of Bath's attitudes and the loathsome hag in the Tale.

The Wife of Bath argues that experience, rather than academic or scriptural texts, should form the basis of that authority and control, especially when it comes to marriage and relationships. As she points out in the Prologue:

> "Experience, though noon auctoritee
> Were in this world, were right ynough to me
> To speke of wo that is in marriage." (lines 1-3)

The Wife of Bath asserts that the only way a marriage can be truly happy is if the wife has control and 'sovereignity' over her husband. She uses her own experience of marriage, especially with her fifth husband, to show how this can be achieved. Her belief in female 'sovereignity' and control is the key theme within her Arthurian romantic tale.

The Wife of Bath's arguments regarding control and the need to base decisions on experience rather than perceived scriptural and textual authority reflects growing contemporary criticism of the Church. At this time, the Bible was only available in Latin. Reformers such as John Wycliffe (English theologian, c. 1320s-1384) were arguing that the Bible should be printed in English so that people could read it and make their own decisions, rather than relying on the Church to translate and explain the teachings of Christ.

FEMINISM

In recent years, *The Wife of Bath's Tale* has often been interpreted as a proto-feminist text given that it focuses so much on the role of women within a relationship, pointing out that it is men that dishonour women. Chaucer writes:

> "Wommen may go saufly up and doun.
> In every bussh or under every tree
> There is noon oother incubus but he,
> And he ne wol doon hem but dishonour."
> (lines 884-887)

In Chaucer's time, the medieval Church was very antifeminist, and encouraged the belief that women should be subservient to their husbands or guardians. Women were seen as lecherous, sexually insatiable, shrewish, superficial and evil. The Wife of Bath is scornful of men who believe that women should be submissive, using scriptural texts as justification for their beliefs. She believes, and vehemently argues, that lack of experience with women is the real reason why such texts are biased against them. During her argument with Jankyn concerning his delight in reading books highlighting women's misdeeds, she is so angered that she tears pages from the book and hits him with it.

Arguments that the Wife of Bath is a truly feminist character are weakened by the fact that she actually conforms to some of those stereotypes, being sexually voracious, dominant, gossipy and shrewish.

PILGRIMAGE

In medieval times, people used to go on pilgrimages to the shrines of saints throughout Europe and to Israel, known as the Holy Land. The Church taught that if they did so, then they could gain forgiveness for sins. Sometimes people went on pilgrimages as a way of atoning for a crime, while other people chose to go on pilgrimages as a way of affirming their religious beliefs. Popular shrines included Walsingham and Canterbury in the UK and Santiago de Compostela in Spain. An increasing trend at this time was for people like the Wife of Bath to deliberately opt to go on pilgrimage, not for any outwardly religious reasons, but as a way of travelling and seeing the world, making them, in effect, medieval tourists. As individual travel was dangerous, they would gather at a specific inn within a major city like London and travel as a group. In *The Canterbury Tales*, the group of pilgrims is socially diverse and includes a prioress, a franklin, a knight, a miller and a reeve. In order to while away the time while travelling, the host and leader of the party proposes that each of them should tell a story.

The lack of piety in which the Wife of Bath regards the concept of a pilgrimage may be a reflection of the increasing contemporary criticism of pilgrimages, which would have been very familiar to Chaucer. The Wife of Bath is a well-travelled pilgrim, having visited Jerusalem, Rome, Bologna, Compostela and Cologne.

LANGUAGE AND STYLE

Chaucer is often regarded as the father of modern English, due to his use of English as a form of written language. His work showed that English could be just as sophisticated, elegant, fun and complex as Latin and French, which were more commonly used during that period. Other people writing in English at this time included Julian of Norwich (English theologian, c. 1342-1416), William Langland (English writer, c. 1332-1386) and John Gower (English poet, c. 1330-1408).

The Canterbury Tales were written as narrative poems. They are among the first secular texts to be written in English, albeit in what is known as Middle English. The language bears some resemblance to modern English; for example, the original first lines of *The Wife of Bath's Tale* read:

> "In th'olde dayes of the Kyng Arthour,
> Of which that Britons speken greet honour,
> All was this land fulfild of fayerye." (lines 863-867)

The actual language used varies considerably, and is one of the greatest strengths of this work of literature. Chaucer demonstrates the way language varies from one social class to another, showing the sheer breadth of language that is available for use. It can be very learned and academic, with lots of references to other authors and texts. On the other hand it can also be very bawdy and lively, as demonstrated in the accounts of the Wife of Bath's relationships with her husband, or when she is talking about sex. Many of the words used are very ordinary, simple words from everyday life such as 'gossip', 'barley-breed' and 'pissed'.

The Prologue is much longer than the Tale itself. The Prologue is made up of 861 lines of continuous verse, while the Tale lasts from lines 862 to 1270.

Alliteration is used extensively throughout *The Wife of Bath's Tale,* especially in terms of the repetition of a similar sound in short phrases, e. g. "lige lady" (line 1037).

Use of simile is also present, allowing indirect comparisons to be made. A good example of this is:

> "And al day after hidde hym as an owle
> So wo was hym, his wyf looked so foule."
> (lines 1087-1089)

Just as an owl comes at night, only in the darkness did the knight feel he could bear to be near his wife.

RHYME

Chaucer introduced the use of rhyme royal into English literature. He is generally thought to have been the first poet to use the a-b-a-b-b-c-c rhyme scheme, a system which has been used by other poets since then, including William Butler Yeats (Irish poet, 1865-1939) and W. H. Auden (English poet, 1907-1973).

EXEMPLUM

The Wife of Bath's Tale is an ideal example of a literary device known as an exemplum. This refers to a story which is designed to illustrate an intellectual concept. Both the Prologue and the Tale itself are dominated by one question: what do women want most in the world? Some of the ideas expressed in *The Wife of Bath's Tale* are clearly influenced by other literature of the period, such as *Roman de la Rose* (c. 1270s) by Jean de Meun (French writer, c. 1240-1305), and the views on celibacy expressed by St Jerome (Roman theologian, c. 347-420) in *Hieronymous contra Jovinianum* (393). The views expressed in the Prologue are demonstrated in the Tale. In the Prologue, an older woman who has lost her beauty describes how she gained control over a younger husband, thus leading to a happy marriage. In the Tale, the young knight has to accept a woman who is not beautiful and is much older as his wife. It is this 'loathsome hag' who sets the tone for the marriage, and demands that her husband acknowledges her rule, before giving him what he wants.

The Tale reverses what the Church and society regard as the natural order. It is Queen Guinevere who takes the initiative, requiring King Arthur to step aside and allow her to make decisions. It is the Queen and her ladies who pass judgement on the knight, rather than other males. The ultimate judgement is based on experience of life, rather than on the authority found within scripture or legal books. Ultimately, the knight has to be redeemed by a 'loathsome hag' after he has committed a crime against a pretty maiden.

KING ARTHUR AND COURTLY LOVE

The theme of courtly love was extremely popular during the medieval period, and features strongly in the literature and culture of the time. Courtly love owes its origins to the work of the troubadours of southern France, who promoted the idea that true love cannot exist within marriage. Instead a spiritual, idealised true love can exist without any sexual relationship, allowing a man to serve the woman he adores without having to marry her. Such love can often be regarded as a torment, especially if the man is away from his lady love, rendering him unable to sleep or eat. This can result in physical changes, making him unrecognizable. Along with this, there had been a renaissance in the popularity of stories of King Arthur and his Knights of the Round Table, who were generally portrayed as noble adventurers who served their chosen lady even if they were not married to her.

By the time this story was written, Arthurian imagery and the concept of courtly love had become prevalent throughout Europe. In *The Wife of Bath's Tale*, the focus is very much on female characters, primarily Queen Guinevere and the 'loathesome hag' who becomes the knight's wife. The Queen is portrayed as wise and powerful, and is able to make decisions of her own even though she first has to seek the permission of her husband to utilise his powers.

Knights were expected to be morally upright and chivalric, displaying 'gentilesse' at all times by keeping promises and behaving virtuously. In the Tale, there is a discussion between the knight and his wife on the subject of gentilesse (lines 1158-1218) and whether it is due to an accident of birth and riches, or whether it is a matter of personal character and a reflection of their actions. During this conversation, the wife points out that "gentillesse cometh fro God allone" (line 1162).

The knight portrayed in *The Wife of Bath's Tale* does not fit any images of chivalry due to the fact that he has raped a young girl. This action has destroyed the image of a knight as being of high moral standing. Nevertheless, as with all Arthurian tales, a quest forms a central part of the story. In this case, the knight is sent on a quest to find an answer to a given question, and unless he succeeds in that quest, he will lose his life.

FURTHER REFLECTION

SOME QUESTIONS TO THINK ABOUT...

- To what extent does the knight's punishment fit the crime?
- Can older women be beautiful? What are the implications of the way this tale portrays older women as ugly by comparison with younger ones?
- How relevant is the issue of 'gentilesse' today?
- In what ways does the Tale reflect the views of the Wife of Bath?
- To what extent is the desire for control in marriage relevant today?
- To what extent do the issues and views expressed in *The Wife of Bath's Prologue and Tale* reflect modern life?
- To what extent do the views expressed in the following quote lead to a happy marriage?

  "My lady and my love, and wyf so deere,
  I put me in youre wise governance.
  Cheseth yourself, which may be moost pleasance

And moost honour to you and me also.
I do no fors the wheither of the two
For as yow liketh, it suffiseth me." (lines 1230-1235)

- What do women really want? Would the same answer be true if this question was asked today?
- To what extent can *The Wife of Bath's Tale* be considered a feminist text?

We want to hear from you!
Leave a comment on your online library
and share your favourite books on social media!

FURTHER READING

REFERENCE EDITION

- Chaucer, G. (1992) *The Canterbury Tales*. London: Everyman.

REFERENCE STUDIES

- Croft, S. ed. (2007) *Oxford Student Texts: Geoffrey Chaucer: The Wife of Bath's Tale*. Oxford: Oxford University Press.

ADAPTATIONS

- *Canturbury Tales*. 'The Wife of Bath'. (2003) [TV episode]. Andy De Emmony. Dir. UK: BBC.

The Wife of Bath's Tale has been translated and rewritten by countless authors over the centuries. There are thousands of different editions available. It has also been made into films, plays and animations.

There is a tourist destination in Canterbury known as The Canterbury Tales (www.canterburytales.org.uk) which includes a retelling of *The Wife of Bath's Tale*. Re-enactors are used to engage with visitors and help bring the tales alive.

www.brightsummaries.com

Ebook EAN: 9782808015516

Paperback EAN: 9782808015523

Legal Deposit: D/2018/12603/534

Cover: © Primento

Digital conception by Primento, the digital partner of
publishers.